The
Beautiful
Mandalas
Coloring Book

The Beautiful Mandalas

Coloring Book

Lovely patterns to calm and delight

SIRIUS

SIRIUS

This edition published in 2023 by Sirius Publishing, a division of
Arcturus Publishing Limited,
26/27 Bickels Yard, 151–153 Bermondsey Street,
London SE1 3HA

ISBN: 978-1-3988-2843-8
CH011123NT
Supplier 29, Date 1222, PI 00003109

Printed in China

Introduction

Taking the form of a wheel or circle, mandalas consist of repeating patterns of symbols. These circular designs occur in many religions, including Buddhism, Hinduism, Shinto, and Jainism, where they are used as a map to show gods, heavenly or spiritual places, and sometimes actual shrines. In Buddhism, a mandala may represent the whole universe, depicted with Mount Meru, the sacred five-peaked mountain of Jain, Hindu, and Buddhist cosmology, at its heart.

Mandalas are most often used to evoke a spiritual journey that begins at their outer edge and which moves through the various layers to arrive at the inner core. The designs gathered here range from the simplest versions to more detailed and complex examples that will test your coloring skill and ability to create a color scheme. Find a peaceful spot, make your color selection, and spend a couple of hours creating your own special mandala.

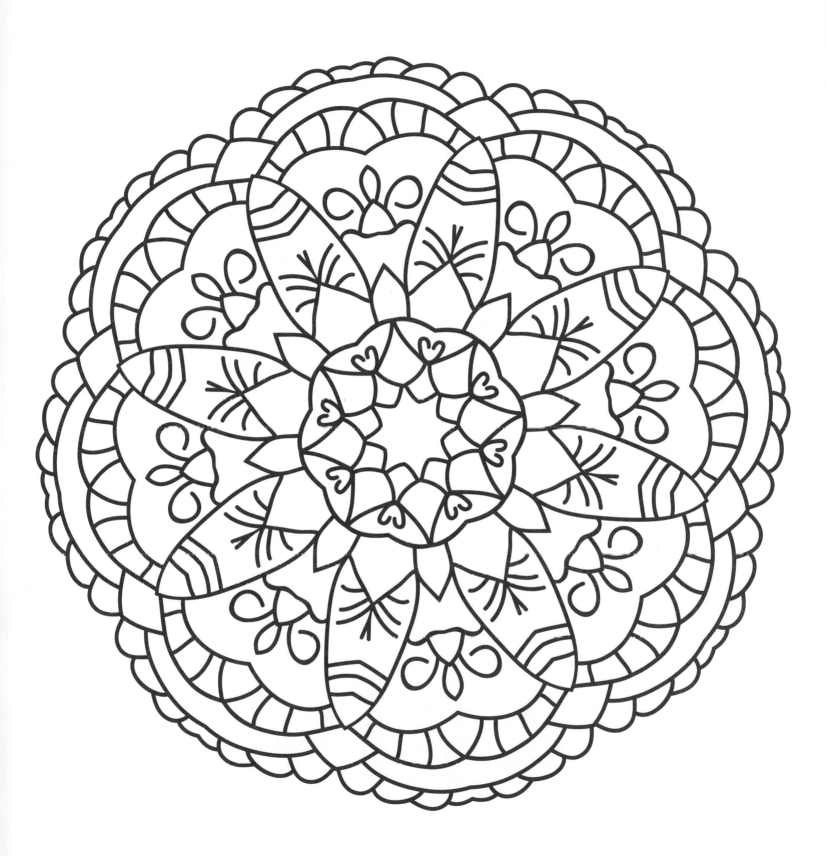